COGAT®
GRADE 3
VERBAL

3 Practice Tests
Level 9

Savant Test Prep™

www.SavantPrep.com

Please leave a review for this book!

Thank you for purchasing this resource.

Please take a moment to leave a
review on the website where you purchased this.

TABLE OF CONTENTS

INTRODUCTION

COGAT® GENERAL INFORMATION

- COGAT® stands for Cognitive Abilities Test®.
- The test measures students' reasoning skills and problem-solving skills.
- It provides educators with an overall assessment of students' academic strengths and weaknesses.
- The COGAT® is commonly used as a screener for gifted and talented programs.
    - Gifted and Talented (G&T) selection sometimes requires a teacher recommendation as well.
- The test is usually administered in a group setting.
- A teacher (or other school associate) administers the test, reading the directions.
- Please check with your school/testing site regarding its testing procedures, as these may differ.

COGAT® LEVEL 9 FORMAT

- Students in third grade take the COGAT® Level 9.
- The test is divided into 3 main parts, each called a "Battery." Each Battery has three question types. See the chart below.

VERBAL BATTERY	NON-VERBAL BATTERY	QUANTITATIVE BATTERY
Verbal Analogies: 22 Questions	Figure Analogies: 20 Questions	Number Puzzles: 16 Questions
Verbal Classification: 20 Questions	Figure Classification: 20 Questions	Number Series: 18 Questions
Sentence Completion: 20 Questions	Paper Folding: 16 Questions	Number Analogies: 18 Questions

- Often, schools administer one Battery per day, allowing approximately 45 minutes per Battery.
- Students have around 15 minutes to complete each question type (for example, students would have around 15 minutes to complete Verbal Analogies).
- See the following pages for examples and explanations of each question type.

COGAT® SCORING

- Students receive points for correct answers. Points are not deducted for incorrect answers. (Therefore, students should at least guess versus leaving a question blank.)
- In general, schools have a "cut-off" COGAT® score, which they consider together with additional criteria, for gifted & talented acceptance. This varies by school.
- This score is usually at least 98%. (However, some schools accept scores of 95% or even 85%.)
- A score of 98% means that your child scored as well as, or better than, 98% of those in his/her testing group.
- COGAT® scores are available for the entire test and can be broken down by Battery.
- Depending on the school/program, such a "cut-off" score may only be required on one or two of the Batteries (and not on the test overall).
- It is essential to check with your school/program for their acceptance procedures.
- The COGAT® Practice Tests in this book can not yield these percentiles because they have not been given to a large enough group of students to produce an accurate comparison/calculation.

HOW TO USE THIS BOOK

1. Go over the Question Examples together with your child. These begin on the next page.

2. Do Practice Test 1 (Workbook Format)
   - Do these questions with your child, especially if this is your child's first exposure to COGAT®-prep questions. These questions have a "workbook format," meaning they are meant to be done together.
   - Do not assign a time limit.
   - Talk about what the question is asking your child to do.
   - Questions progress in difficulty. (The first few questions are quite simple.)
   - Go over the answers using the Answer Key.
   - For questions missed, go over the answers again, discussing what makes the correct answer better than the other choices.

3. Do the remaining Practice Tests following Practice Test 1.
   - If your child progressed easily through Practice Test 1, see how well they can do without your help.
   - If your child needed assistance with much of Practice Test 1, then continue to assist your child with Practice Test 2.
   - If you wish to assign a time limit, assign around 15 minutes per question type.
   - Go over the answers using the Answer Key.
   - For questions missed, go over the answers again, discussing what makes the correct answer better than the other choices.

4. Need more practice?

- **Get 300+ new questions per book.**

- **Check out Savant Test Prep™ books on Amazon®.**

TEST-TAKING TIPS

- Ensure your child listens carefully to the directions, especially in the Sentence Completion section.
- Make sure (s)he does not rush through questions. (There is no prize for finishing first!) Tell your child to look carefully at the question. Then, tell your child to look at each answer choice before marking his/her answer.
  - If you notice your child continuing to rush through the questions, tell him/her to point to each part of the question. Then, point to each answer choice.
- If (s)he does not know the answer, then use the process of elimination. Cross out any answer choices which are clearly incorrect, then choose from those remaining.
- This tip/suggestion is entirely at your discretion. You may wish to offer some sort of special motivation to encourage your child to do his/her best. An extra incentive of, for example, an art set, a building block set, or a special outing can go a long way in motivating young learners!
- The night before testing, make sure your child has enough sleep, without any interruptions. (Think about the difference in **your** brain function with a good night's sleep vs. without. The same goes for your child's.)
- The morning before the test, ensure your child eats a healthy breakfast with protein and complex carbs. Do not let them eat sugar, chocolate, etc.
- If you can choose the time your child will take the test (for example, if (s)he will take the test individually, instead of at school with a group), opt for a morning testing session, when your child will be most alert.

QUESTION EXAMPLES

- Here is an overview of the COGAT® question types.
- This section has <u>simple</u> examples, to introduce your child to test concepts.
  - Do these examples together with your child.
- Below the questions are explanations for parents.

1. VERBAL ANALOGIES (VERBAL BATTERY)

• **Directions (read to child):** Here are two sets of words. Look at the first set of words. Try to see how they belong together. Then, look at the next set of words. The question mark shows where the answer is missing. Can you see which answer choice would make the second set of words go together in the same way that the first set of words goes together?

scales → fish : feathers → ?   A. pen   B. shark   C. beak   D. bird   E. fly

• **Explanation (for parents):** Figure out how the first set is related and belongs together. Then, (s)he must figure out which answer choice would go with the first word of the second set so that the second set would have the same analogous relationship as the first set. (The small arrows demonstrate that the words go together.)

• **Strategy 1:** Define a "rule" to describe how the first set belongs together. Then, take this "rule" and use it with the second set. Look at the answer choices, and figure out which answer would make the second set follow your "rule."

• **Using the above question as an example, say to your child:**
In this question, we have "scales" and "fish." Scales are part of a fish. Also, more specifically, scales cover a fish. A rule would be, "the first thing covers the second thing." In the second set we have "feathers." Let's try the answer choices with our rule. A pen, shark, beak, or fly is not correct. "Bird" is correct because feathers cover a bird.

• **Strategy 2:** Come up with a sentence to describe how the first set belongs together. Then, use this sentence with the second word. Look at the answer choices, and figure out which answer would make the sentence work with this second set. With both strategies, if more than one answer choice works, then you need a more specific rule/sentence.

• Make sure your child does not choose an answer simply because it *has to do with* the previous words or reminds them of previous words. In the above example, "beak" *has to do with* "feathers." "Shark" may *remind* them of the second word in the first set, "fish." These types of words are sometimes included in the answer choices, and students who do not look carefully at the question may choose them by mistake.

• The examples on the next page outline some of the logic used in analogy questions.

• **Directions:** The first set of words goes together in some way. In the second set of words, one word is missing. Which answer choice would make the second set of words go together in the same way that the first set goes together? (Note: the answer and logic are below the question.)

Question	Answer Choices			
1. Spider -is to- Web as Bird -is to- ? *Answer - Nest (Animal: Animal's Home)*	Flower	Bench	Nest	Bird
2. Acorns -are to- Squirrel as Seeds -are to- ? *Answer - Bird (Animal: Animal's Food)*	Grass	Bird	Fish	Snake
3. Calf -is to- Cow as Cub -is to- ? *Answer - Tiger (Animal Baby: Animal Adult)*	Tiger	Horse	Goose	Bull
4. Small -is to- Little as Afraid -is to- ? *Answer - Scared (Synonyms)*	Dark	Tired	Haunted	Scared
5. Happy -is to- Sad as Wet -is to- ? *Answer - Dry (Opposites)*	Damp	Clean	Water	Dry
6. Tiger -is to- Cheetah as Butterfly -is to- ? *Answer - Moth (Similar: Similar (Flying Insects))*	Bird	Bat	Moth	Jaguar
7. Flower -is to- Bouquet as Kernel -is to- ? *Answer - Corn Cob (Part: Whole)*	Snack	Plant	Corn Cob	Crop
8. Ship -is to- Port as Car -is to- ? *Answer - Garage (Object: Location)*	Truck	Garage	Marina	Wheel
9. Pencil -is to- Paper as Paint -is to- ? *Answer - Wall (Object: Object Used With)*	Wall	Color	Red	Light
10. Lumber -is to- Fence as Paper -is to- ? *Answer - Book (Object: Product That Object Is Put Together To Make)*	Log	Branch	Tree	Book
11. Cheese -is to- Refrigerator as Ice -is to- ? *Answer - Freezer (Object: Item Used to Store/Hold Object)*	Snow	Toaster	Freezer	Cube
12. Box -is to- Cube as Globe -is to- ? *Answer - Sphere (Object: Similar Shape)*	Prism	Sphere	Oval	Pentagon
13. Straw -is to- Juice as Spoon -is to- ? *Answer - Cereal (Utensil: Object Utensil Is Used With)*	Cereal	Salad	Steak	Sandwich
14. Egg -is to- Chicken as Milk -is to- ? *Answer - Cow (Food/Drink: Source of Food/Drink)*	Chick	Cheese	Rooster	Cow
15. Ambulance -is to- Paramedic as Tractor -is to- ? *Answer - Farmer (Object/Vehicle: User)*	Doctor	Teacher	Scientist	Farmer
16. Large -is to- Enormous as Good -is to- ? *Answer - Super (Adjective: Higher Degree of Adjective)*	Bad	So-so	Happy	Super
17. Rose -is to- Flower as Ant -is to- ? *Answer - Insect (Specific Type: Group)*	Insect	Spider	Anthill	Beetle

2. VERBAL CLASSIFICATION (VERBAL BATTERY)

• **Directions (read to child):** The three words in the top row are alike in some way. Look at the bottom row. There are five words. Which word in the bottom row goes best with the three words in the top row?

red   **green**   **blue**

A. paint   B. color   C. white   D. rainbow   E. shade

• **Explanation (for parents):** Together with your child, try to figure out a "rule" describing how the top words are alike and belong together. Then, apply the "rule" to each answer choice to determine which one follows it. If your child finds that more than one choice follows the rule, then a more specific rule is needed.

• **Using the above question as an example, say to your child:** In the top row, we have "red," "green," and "blue." What do these have in common? Each of these are colors. This is how they are alike. Which answer choice follows this rule of "colors?" The only answer choice that does is "white."

• Make sure your child does not choose a word simply because the choice *has to do with* the top three. For example, the other choices, especially Choice B ("color") have to do with the top three. However, "white" is the only choice that actually follows the rule.

Here is another example to demonstrate the importance of "rules" that are *specific*.

Atlantic   **Indian**   **Arctic**

A. American   B. Caribbean Sea   C. East Coast   D. Pacific   E. ocean

In this example, the correct rule is "oceans of the world." (The world's oceans are the: Atlantic, Pacific, Arctic, Indian, and Southern.)

However, a test-taker may at first come up with the rule "large body of water." If this happens, (s)he would have more than one answer choice that could be correct (Caribbean Sea or Pacific).

In this case, a more specific rule is needed. Here, (s)he should read the top three words again. In doing so, (s)he may realize that the top three words are large bodies of water that are *also* oceans.

A more specific rule would be "ocean" or "oceans of the world." Therefore, the correct answer would be Choice D, "Pacific."

• **Directions (read to child):** I am going to read you a group of words. The words go together in some way. Let's figure out how the words go together. Then, I will read you another group of words. Let's figure out which one from this group goes best with the words in the first group.

(Parent note: the answer and logic are below the question.)

Question		Answer Choices			

1. Cave   Hive   Web | Spider   Nest   Vet   Bat
Answer - Nest (Animal Homes)

2. Butterfly   Ant   Bee | Worm   Horse   Bird   Dragonfly
Answer - Dragonfly (Animal Types (Insects))

3. Forest   Jungle   Desert | Tree   Valley   Rainforest   City
Answer - Rainforest (Habitats)

4. Lemon   Grape   Apple | Strawberry   Farm   Sweet   Lettuce
Answer - Strawberry (Kinds of Food (Fruit))

5. Scientist   Nurse   Detective | Superhero   Teenager   Pilot   Fairy
Answer - Pilot (Jobs)

6. Sock   Skate   Boot | Slipper   Cap   Mitten   Toe
Answer - Slipper (Objects Worn On Feet)

7. Hot Air Balloon   Jet   Helicopter | Ship   Airport   Bird   Airplane
Answer - Airplane (Vehicles for Air Travel)

8. Ruler   Measuring Tape   Scale | Thermometer   TV   Pen   Number
Answer - Thermometer (Object Use (Used to Measure))

9. Pillow   Blanket   Mattress | Towel   Chair   Sheet   Table
Answer - Sheet (Object Location (Found on Beds))

10. Fire   Sun   Stove | Cookie   Toaster   Beach   Camp
Answer - Toaster (Object Characteristics (Provide Heat))

11. Planet   Ball   Globe | Country   Goal   Bubble   Racetrack
Answer - Bubble (Object Shape (Spherical))

3. SENTENCE COMPLETION (VERBAL BATTERY)

• **Directions (read to child):** First, read the sentence. There is a missing word. Which answer choice goes best in the sentence? (Read the sentences and choices to your child. They may read along silently.)

As the water slowly evaporated, the bird bath became _____.

A. wet   B. empty   C. full   D. damp   E. clean

• **Explanation** Here, your child must use the information in the question and make inferences (i.e., make a best guess based on the information) and choose the *best* answer choice to fill in the blank.

• Note that Sentence Completion questions do not solely test vocabulary, but reasoning skills as well.

• Make sure your child pays close attention to every word in the sentence and to every answer choice. Have him/her re-read the complete sentence with the answer choice to ensure their choice makes the *most* sense compared to the other choices (the answer is B).

• Tell him/her to pay special attention to "negative" words like "not" or "no." Also, (s)he should watch out for words like "though," "although," "even though," which would show contrasting ideas.

Parents, read the below with your child.

Watch out!

This book is filled with tricky questions. Can you answer them?

Of course you can!

Pay close attention to each question and try your best.

We'll be here to help you along the way!

10

COGAT® PRACTICE TEST 1
(WORKBOOK FORMAT)

VERBAL ANALOGIES

What's missing?

Sara

Directions (Read these aloud to your child. Your child may read along silently): The first set of words goes together in some way. In the second set of words, one word is missing. You must figure out which answer choice would go in place of the question mark so that the second set of words goes together in the same way that the first set of words goes together.

Explanation (for parents): A more detailed explanation and another example question is on p.6. If you have not already, look over p.6. Following is an excerpt. Your child must figure out how the first set of words is related and belongs together. Then, (s)he must figure out which answer choice would replace the question mark so that the second set would have the same relationship as the first set.

Example (read this to child): "Soft" and "hard." These are the words in the first set. (Together, try to come up with a "rule" describing how they are alike and go together.) The opposite of soft is hard. So, the rule is that the two words are opposites. Let's look at the first word in the second set: "deep." Next, let's carefully look at each answer choice. Remembering our rule, which choice goes best with "deep?" What is the opposite of deep? "Shallow."

1   **soft → hard : deep → ?**

    Ⓐ shallow   Ⓑ ocean   Ⓒ wide   Ⓓ narrow   Ⓔ heavy

2   **microscope → scientist : whistle → ?**

    Ⓐ doctor   Ⓑ nurse   Ⓒ astronaut   Ⓓ referee   Ⓔ player

3 deck → card : flower → ?

   A gift   B florist   C petal   D leaf   E bouquet

4 hour → day : word → ?

   A envelope   B stamp   C mailbox   D alphabet   E sentence

5 cow → milk : sheep → ?

   A hay   B wool   C farm   D fleece   E lamb

6 scissors → cut : sponge → ?

   A wipe   B water   C measure   D kitchen   E tub

7 jog → run : stroll → ?

   A stand   B end   C walk   D begin   E pause

8 chilly → freezing : misty → ?

  Ⓐ dark   Ⓑ sunny   Ⓒ foggy   Ⓓ cold   Ⓔ mystery

9 bow → arrow : hammer → ?

  Ⓐ wrench   Ⓑ target   Ⓒ door   Ⓓ nail   Ⓔ tool

10 violin → instrument : rose → ?

  Ⓐ red   Ⓑ tulip   Ⓒ petal   Ⓓ perfume   Ⓔ flower

11 saw → cut : needle → ?

  Ⓐ stitch   Ⓑ cloth   Ⓒ button   Ⓓ sharp   Ⓔ fabric

12 author → write : baker → ?

  Ⓐ flour   Ⓑ dough   Ⓒ bread   Ⓓ cook   Ⓔ oven

13   pour → water : spend → ?

    A drink   B idea   C food   D dizzy   E money

14   feather → bird : city → ?

    A state   B street   C river   D town   E farmer

15   silent → quiet : starving → ?

    A thirsty   B full   C hungry   D food   E craving

16   whale → mammal : lizard → ?

    A snake   B reptile   C gecko   D fish   E alligator

17   lock → key : toothpaste → ?

    A tube   B mouth   C cavity   D dentist   E toothbrush

18 dusk → dawn : entrance → ?

Ⓐ opening   Ⓑ key   Ⓒ exit   Ⓓ door   Ⓔ closed

19 fire → smoke : sun → ?

Ⓐ shine   Ⓑ bright   Ⓒ shadow   Ⓓ heat   Ⓔ summer

20 bright → glowing : dim → ?

Ⓐ light   Ⓑ dark   Ⓒ clear   Ⓓ gray   Ⓔ cloudy

21 pen → write : chalk → ?

Ⓐ erase   Ⓑ break   Ⓒ board   Ⓓ draw   Ⓔ dust

22 win → lose : grow → ?

Ⓐ keep   Ⓑ stretch   Ⓒ spread   Ⓓ stand   Ⓔ shrink

VERBAL CLASSIFICATION

Which one goes best?

Kai

Directions (Read these aloud to your child. Your child may read along silently): The top row has three words that are alike in some way. In the bottom row are five words. Which word in the bottom row goes best with the words in the top row?

Explanation (for parents): A more detailed explanation and another Verbal Classification example question is on p.8. If you have not already, look over p.8. Following is an excerpt. Together with your child, try to figure out a "rule" describing how the top words are alike and belong together. Then, apply the "rule" to each answer choice to determine which one follows it. If your child finds that more than one choice follows the rule, then a more specific rule is needed.

Example (read to child): In the top row are the words "rose," "tulip," and "daisy." Let's come up with a "rule" to describe how these are each alike or how they belong together. These are all types of flowers. Now, let's find the answer choice on the bottom that follows this same rule of "flowers."

We have "tree," "sunflower," "leaf," "vine," and "fern." "Sunflower" follows our rule because it is a type of flower. The rest are types of plants or parts of plants, but they are not a type of flower.

1   **rose   tulip   daisy**

     A tree   B sunflower   C leaf   D vine   E fern

2   **pencil   marker   crayon**

     A eraser   B ink   C paintbrush   D notebook   E paper

3   Sun   fire   lava

- (A) red
- (B) warm
- (C) smoke
- (D) yellow
- (E) candle

4   guitar   harp   violin

- (A) cello
- (B) drum
- (C) instrument
- (D) tuba
- (E) flute

5   fork   knife   chopsticks

- (A) dish
- (B) cup
- (C) bowl
- (D) spoon
- (E) plate

6   lion   tiger   leopard

- (A) bear
- (B) wolf
- (C) elephant
- (D) jaguar
- (E) panda

7   Paris   London   Rome

- (A) continent
- (B) Japan
- (C) country
- (D) New York
- (E) Asia

8   **couch**   **chair**   **stool**

A living room   B lamp   C table   D floor   E recliner

9   **Mercury**   **Venus**   **Earth**

A sun   B Jupiter   C moon   D planet   E asteroid

10   **square**   **triangle**   **circle**

A shape   B angle   C point   D line   E rectangle

11   **doctor**   **nurse**   **surgeon**

A hospital   B dentist   C patient   D artist   E mechanic

12   **shark**   **whale**   **dolphin**

A pig   B ocean   C horse   D seal   E seaweed

13 **hammer**   **wrench**   **screwdriver**

Ⓐ toolbox   Ⓑ saw   Ⓒ pencil   Ⓓ vacuum   Ⓔ broom

14 **mountain**   **hill**   **volcano**

Ⓐ ridge   Ⓑ river   Ⓒ lake   Ⓓ cave   Ⓔ rock

15 **cherry**   **lemon**   **apple**

Ⓐ pumpkin   Ⓑ grape   Ⓒ pear   Ⓓ strawberry   Ⓔ blueberry

16 **detective**   **police officer**   **security guard**

Ⓐ doctor   Ⓑ dentist   Ⓒ waiter   Ⓓ salesperson   Ⓔ sheriff

17 **goldfish**   **tuna**   **salmon**

Ⓐ seahorse   Ⓑ whale   Ⓒ crab   Ⓓ trout   Ⓔ octopus

18 oak elm maple

    A vine   B tulip   C pine   D forest   E tree

19 hour minute second

    A day   B clock   C time   D morning   E midnight

20 North Pole Antarctica Alaska

    A snow   B glacier   C iceberg   D Arctic   E Mexico

21 happy joyful excited

    A grin   B awake   C tired   D sad   E cheerful

22 tennis basketball golf

    A game   B goal   C player   D ball   E soccer

SENTENCE COMPLETION

Think carefully!

Maya

1 **The baby birds chirped loudly when they were ____.**

   Ⓐ silent   Ⓑ hungry   Ⓒ quiet   Ⓓ full   Ⓔ calm

2 **The sun was so bright that I had to ____ my eyes.**

   Ⓐ shine   Ⓑ view   Ⓒ cover   Ⓓ light   Ⓔ see

3 **She wore a jacket because the weather was ____.**

   Ⓐ warm   Ⓑ humid   Ⓒ hot   Ⓓ dry   Ⓔ chilly

4 **The path was slippery due to the ____.**

   Ⓐ rain   Ⓑ length   Ⓒ park   Ⓓ forest   Ⓔ animals

5   The explorers needed a map so they wouldn't get ____ in the jungle.

A directions   B lost   C tired   D treasure   E hungry

6   Despite his fear of heights, Leo ____ the ladder to get to the roof.

A lowered   B removed   C dropped   D climbed   E took down

7   The detective ____ the clues in order to solve the mystery.

A skipped   B examined   C misplaced   D erased   E hid

8   After months of training, she finally ____ the championship race.

A completed   B avoided   C viewed   D cheered   E watched

9   The student ____ the math problem correctly, so there was no need to raise his hand for help.

A missed   B skipped   C misunderstood   D forgot   E solved

10   The strong wind ____ the leaves of the trees.

   Ⓐ collected   Ⓑ threw   Ⓒ scattered   Ⓓ gathered   Ⓔ froze

11   We had to ____ our camping trip because of the heavy rain.

   Ⓐ plan   Ⓑ extend   Ⓒ ignore   Ⓓ postpone   Ⓔ celebrate

12   She tried to ____ her excitement, but her big smile gave it away.

   Ⓐ show   Ⓑ display   Ⓒ conceal   Ⓓ release   Ⓔ express

13   The hikers reached the ____ of the mountain after a long climb up.

   Ⓐ base   Ⓑ summit   Ⓒ foot   Ⓓ beginning   Ⓔ deep

14   We could hear strong thunder in the distance, warning us that a storm was ____.

   Ⓐ ending   Ⓑ forming   Ⓒ vanishing   Ⓓ tiny   Ⓔ weak

15 The actor was nervous before stepping on stage, but he _____ his fear and performed well.

A controlled   B strengthened   C raised   D increased   E revealed

16 To _____ correct results, the scientist repeated the experiment three times.

A block   B invent   C imagine   D guess   E confirm

17 She had to _____ the puzzle pieces before putting them together.

A miss   B recycle   C skip   D organize   E cover

18 The teacher _____ the instructions before the test began.

A whispered   B explained   C ignored   D erased   E guessed

19 He carefully _____ the vase to avoid dropping it.

A admired   B lifted   C looked at   D broke   E watched

20 **The fire hoses allowed the firefighters to quickly ____ the fire.**

(A) escape   (B) wash   (C) extinguish   (D) expand   (E) continue

- End of Practice Test 1 (Workbook Format) -

Zoe

COGAT® PRACTICE TEST 2

The first set of words goes together in some way. Which answer choice would go in place of the question mark so that the second set goes together in the same way as the first set?

1   **lion → roar : frog → ?**

     (A) croak   (B) hop   (C) tadpole   (D) slither   (E) squeal

2   **buckle → belt : button → ?**

     (A) shoe   (B) zipper   (C) sock   (D) scarf   (E) shirt

3   **Texas → state : Asia → ?**

     (A) country   (B) continent   (C) ocean   (D) island   (E) equator

4   **ruler → length : clock → ?**

     (A) second   (B) number   (C) time   (D) tick   (E) dial

5   **beak → bird : hoof → ?**

     (A) fish   (B) goat   (C) cat   (D) bat   (E) claw

6. **ocean → sea : canyon → ?**

   A peninsula   B river   C cave   D valley   E peak

7. **dolphin → whale : goldfish → ?**

   A trout   B bird   C guppy   D rabbit   E turtle

8. **gram → weight : meter → ?**

   A volume   B mass   C cup   D distance   E temperature

9. **eyes → see : nose → ?**

   A scent   B taste   C mouth   D nostril   E smell

10. **bicycle → motorcycle : wagon → ?**

    A tricycle   B horse   C race car   D subway   E truck

11   orchestra → conductor : ship's crew → ?

    (A) passenger   (B) boat   (C) president   (D) captain   (E) fisherman

12   phone → battery : refrigerator → ?

    (A) table   (B) electricity   (C) candle   (D) light   (E) switch

13   knight → night : flour → ?

    (A) food   (B) petal   (C) flower   (D) grain   (E) recipe

14   chapter → book : actor → ?

    (A) cast   (B) director   (C) program   (D) title   (E) lines

15   seaweed → ocean : cactus → ?

    (A) plant   (B) desert   (C) swamp   (D) park   (E) farm

16   warm → hot : breezy → ?

   A fast   B rainy   C messy   D windy   E still

17   teacher → classroom : mayor → ?

   A law   B election   C city   D president   E state

18   bee → swarm : star → ?

   A sun   B moon   C galaxy   D sky   E planet

19   push → pull : rise → ?

   A fall   B sunset   C wake up   D wave   E leave

20   orange → carrot : brown → ?

   A lettuce   B black   C vegetable   D pumpkin   E honey

21 director → movie : pilot → ?

(A) airport   (B) flight   (C) seat   (D) wings   (E) vacation

22 sundial → clock : compass → ?

(A) west   (B) map   (C) south   (D) arrow   (E) GPS

Nice Work!

Daniel

1   **red**   **blue**   **green**

A marker   B paint   C crayon   D orange   E color

2   **apartment**   **cabin**   **mansion**

A bridge   B barn   C highway   D cottage   E ferry

3   **Spanish**   **German**   **Japanese**

A Korean   B Mexico   C Asia   D Canada   E Tokyo

4   **touch**   **smell**   **taste**

A blink   B feel   C walk   D jump   E sing

5   **alarm clock**   **grandfather clock**   **hourglass**

A ruler   B number   C stopwatch   D sand   E table

6   **mitten**   **ring**   **bracelet**

Ⓐ sandal   Ⓑ scarf   Ⓒ belt   Ⓓ boot   Ⓔ glove

7   **highway**   **street**   **road**

Ⓐ speed   Ⓑ parking lot   Ⓒ car   Ⓓ freeway   Ⓔ construction

8   **moon**   **comet**   **planet**

Ⓐ spaceship   Ⓑ water   Ⓒ meteor   Ⓓ telescope   Ⓔ orbit

9   **cup**   **thermos**   **bottle**

Ⓐ mug   Ⓑ plate   Ⓒ water   Ⓓ straw   Ⓔ tray

10   **Atlantic**   **Pacific**   **Indian**

Ⓐ Nile   Ⓑ gulf   Ⓒ Arctic   Ⓓ peninsula   Ⓔ Amazon

11 **sidewalk**   **path**   **crosswalk**

A bricks   B trail   C highway   D map   E signal

12 **laughing**   **smiling**   **giggling**

A frowning   B crying   C chuckling   D snoring   E yawning

13 **skates**   **shoes**   **stockings**

A mittens   B pants   C jackets   D scarves   E socks

14 **lion**   **tiger**   **cheetah**

A wolf   B kitten   C elephant   D leopard   E zebra

15 **grape**   **banana**   **tomato**

A watermelon   B fruit   C pumpkin   D vegetable   E cherry

16   **jog**   **skip**   **run**

(A) sprint   (B) think   (C) sleep   (D) nod   (E) stretch

17   **stand**   **rest**   **lean**

(A) swim   (B) sit   (C) crawl   (D) sofa   (E) reach

18   **peacock**   **ostrich**   **hawk**

(A) bat   (B) robin   (C) frog   (D) butterfly   (E) feather

19   **juice**   **vinegar**   **syrup**

(A) pancake   (B) cheese   (C) sugar   (D) caffeine   (E) coffee

20   **turtle**   **clam**   **snail**

(A) catfish   (B) frog   (C) shark   (D) oyster   (E) octopus

SENTENCE COMPLETION
A word in the sentence is missing. Which choice best completes the sentence?

1   As the ____ wind howled through the trees, branches snapped and fell to the ground.

A gentle   B powerful   C soft   D slow   E peaceful

2   After his injury, Scott had a sudden memory ____, forgetting simple details from his day.

A loss   B recovery   C concentration   D gain   E boost

3   Mangoes are a good source of ____ like Vitamin A, which help keep the body healthy.

A sugar   B sweetness   C nutrients   D flavors   E taste

4   When borrowing money, you must ____ what you owe.

A loan   B lend   C spend   D repay   E donate

5   Unlike the village she once called home, Alli found the ____ city much too noisy.

A peaceful   B relaxing   C quiet   D calm   E bustling

6 The symmetry of ice crystals and the hexagon shape of snowflakes are examples of ____ patterns found in nature.

A colorful   B uneven   C mathematical   D musical   E imaginary

7 The mighty walls were meant to ____ people from entering the fortress.

A prevent   B assist   C simplify   D guide   E allow

8 Rushing to the amusement park and finding it closed for the day made them ____.

A thrilled   B relieved   C hopeful   D frustrated   E enthusiastic

9 As a ____ event, all people will be invited to buy a ticket.

A private   B packed   C public   D free   E closed

10 Seeing the Grand Canyon for the first time was an ____ experience beyond anything I had imagined.

A expected   B imagined   C ordinary   D incredible   E average

11 During past droughts, people had to ____ water so there would be enough for drinking and farming.

A conserve B empty C drain D consume E waste

12 The painter's ____ artwork left viewers confused about its meaning.

A beautiful B framed C normal D simple E unusual

13 While studying his family tree last week, Jake found out that a famous king from the 1700s was his ____.

A ancestor B descendant C grandfather D judge E president

14 The decision to move was ____, so we won't be going back to our old house.

A temporary B permanent C brief D trial E short

15 Penguins can ____ in low temperatures in Antarctica because of thick layers of fat and feathers.

A escape B survive C avoid D freeze E increase

16 The town has been ____ for several weeks because everyone left.

(A) popular   (B) crowded   (C) lively   (D) deserted   (E) hectic

17 The entrance to the museum and the gift shop are ____, making it easy for visitors to explore both.

(A) remote   (B) closed   (C) connected   (D) distant   (E) blocked

18 To adopt a pet, people get a letter of ____ from the pet's original owner.

(A) print   (B) refusal   (C) return   (D) welcome   (E) approval

19 Heavy rainfall caused the lake to ____ to twice its previous size.

(A) shrink   (B) expand   (C) dry up   (D) remain   (E) freeze

20 The captain must ____ the ship safely through the storm.

(A) steer   (B) abandon   (C) hide   (D) delay   (E) halt

COGAT® PRACTICE TEST 3

The first set of words goes together in some way. Which answer choice would go in place of the question mark so that the second set goes together in the same way as the first set?

1   **chef → restaurant : doctor → ?**

　　　　　A dentist　　　　B hospital　　　　C sick　　　　D nurse　　　　E surgery

2   **tongue → taste : hand → ?**

　　　　　A touch　　　　B smell　　　　C foot　　　　D wave　　　　E clap

3   **fur → bear : scales → ?**

　　　　　A frog　　　　B skin　　　　C snail　　　　D fish　　　　E dolphin

4   **Atlantic → Europe : Pacific → ?**

　　　　　A Africa　　　　B France　　　　C Canada　　　　D Asia　　　　E China

5   **cube → square : sphere → ?**

　　　　　A clock　　　　B circle　　　　C angle　　　　D rectangle　　　　E triangle

6   roof → house : peak → ?

   A tree   B top   C porch   D valley   E mountain

7   eagle → falcon : whale → ?

   A dolphin   B octopus   C jellyfish   D coral   E shark

8   liquid → liter : time → ?

   A minute   B clock   C calendar   D stopwatch   E alarm

9   happiness → sadness : huge → ?

   A medium   B shrink   C large   D tiny   E grow

10   narrow → wide : build → ?

   A tall   B plan   C destroy   D measure   E short

11   **Canada → Mexico : India → ?**

      Ⓐ South America   Ⓑ Africa   Ⓒ Asia   Ⓓ China   Ⓔ New York

12   **rose → flower : maple → ?**

      Ⓐ leaf   Ⓑ tree   Ⓒ bee   Ⓓ bark   Ⓔ grass

13   **bat → mammal : crocodile → ?**

      Ⓐ amphibian   Ⓑ lizard   Ⓒ reptile   Ⓓ fish   Ⓔ bird

14   **train → subway : horse → ?**

      Ⓐ saddle   Ⓑ carriage   Ⓒ farm   Ⓓ hay   Ⓔ mane

15   **saw → knife : microwave → ?**

      Ⓐ oven   Ⓑ refrigerator   Ⓒ fire   Ⓓ freezer   Ⓔ heat

16   **cotton → fabric : tree → ?**

    A forest   B oak   C logs   D branch   E sand

17   **single → one : triple → ?**

    A triplets   B twin   C two   D three   E pair

18   **grape → vine : cherry → ?**

    A fruit   B tree   C vegetable   D flower   E farm

19   **letter → envelope : cereal → ?**

    A milk   B grain   C breakfast   D bowl   E flakes

20   **poem → poet : painting → ?**

    A museum   B paint   C painter   D reader   E visitor

21 glasses → see : headphones → ?

Ⓐ listen   Ⓑ music   Ⓒ volume   Ⓓ watch   Ⓔ sound

22 heat → sweat : cold → ?

Ⓐ freeze   Ⓑ coat   Ⓒ ice   Ⓓ frost   Ⓔ shiver

Great job! Let's do some more!

Which word on the bottom row goes best with the words on the top row?

1   **North America**   **South America**   **Africa**

     A Europe   *B* Brazil   *C* Canada   *D* Arctic   *E* Pacific

2   **apple**   **banana**   **grape**

     A lettuce   *B* watermelon   *C* onion   *D* cucumber   *E* pepper

3   **book**   **magazine**   **menu**

     A mailbox   *B* internet   *C* website   *D* newspaper   *E* words

4   **ankle**   **hip**   **thigh**

     A wrist   *B* elbow   *C* waist   *D* shoulder   *E* knee

5   **scarf**   **hat**   **mittens**

     A jacket   *B* flip flops   *C* umbrella   *D* tank top   *E* shorts

6   **week**   **day**   **month**

   Ⓐ calendar   Ⓑ year   Ⓒ spring   Ⓓ summer   Ⓔ April

7   **flashlight**   **lantern**   **headlamp**

   Ⓐ battery   Ⓑ electricity   Ⓒ shine   Ⓓ candle   Ⓔ glow

8   **mermaid**   **wizard**   **witch**

   Ⓐ fireman   Ⓑ astronaut   Ⓒ fairy   Ⓓ pilot   Ⓔ magician

9   **chilly**   **frosty**   **cold**

   Ⓐ freezing   Ⓑ temperature   Ⓒ snow   Ⓓ snowman   Ⓔ season

10   **done**   **finished**   **over**

   Ⓐ begin   Ⓑ ended   Ⓒ start   Ⓓ race   Ⓔ lap

11 **word**   **sentence**   **paragraph**

A author   B edit   C speech   D voice   E chapter

12 **quick**   **speedy**   **swift**

A rabbit   B car   C slow   D rapid   E cheetah

13 **jet**   **helicopter**   **rocket**

A hot air balloon   B outer space   C race car   D bird   E speedboat

14 **basement**   **cellar**   **base**

A middle   B level   C bottom   D ceiling   E mountain

15 **ice**   **frost**   **hail**

A melt   B water   C steam   D snow   E fog

16   **unicycle**   **scooter**   **bicycle**

Ⓐ cargo ship   Ⓑ cruise ship   Ⓒ subway   Ⓓ bus   Ⓔ skateboard

17   **lemon**   **grapefruit**   **orange**

Ⓐ strawberry   Ⓑ fruit   Ⓒ banana   Ⓓ watermelon   Ⓔ lime

18   **lettuce**   **cucumber**   **broccoli**

Ⓐ vegetable   Ⓑ carrot   Ⓒ cherry   Ⓓ salad   Ⓔ salt

19   **butter**   **yogurt**   **cheese**

Ⓐ peanuts   Ⓑ juice   Ⓒ pasta   Ⓓ ice cream   Ⓔ bread

20   **lock**   **password**   **guard**

Ⓐ curtain   Ⓑ number   Ⓒ fence   Ⓓ book   Ⓔ table

SENTENCE COMPLETION

A word in the sentence is missing. Which choice best completes the sentence?

1 **This microscope allows us to see ____ details on objects that are normally invisible to us.**

A large B distant C tiny D enormous E fantasy

2 **The river was flowing at a ____ of 10 miles per hour, making it dangerous to swim in.**

A rate B drip C sprinkle D trickle E puddle

3 **I will ____ the stray kitten carefully, so it doesn't get scared and run away.**

A ignore B shove C drop D approach E avoid

4 **As the number of ____ increased, the small fishing community became a busy port town.**

A states B forests C farms D mountains E visitors

5 **Water is an ____ resource for all living things to survive.**

A unnecessary B optional C essential D extra E unimportant

6 I can always ____ on my older brother to help me with my homework.

(A) look down   (B) depend   (C) pass   (D) try   (E) hesitate

7 If he wants to do well on the exam, he must ____ studying instead of quitting early.

(A) pause   (B) continue   (C) avoid   (D) cease   (E) settle

8 The mountain climber will need time to ____ her strength before attempting another climb.

(A) weaken   (B) reduce   (C) break   (D) rebuild   (E) strain

9 Even though I am the oldest in my family, I am the ____.

(A) shortest   (B) older   (C) wisest   (D) younger   (E) youngest

10 Because this bridge is over deep water, it was built to stay ____ in strong winds.

(A) shaky   (B) cracked   (C) damaged   (D) uneven   (E) firm

11   The heat here is so ____ that people often stay indoors during the afternoon.

   A extreme   B mild   C pleasant   D moderate   E refreshing

12   The scientist enjoys learning about ____ species that no longer exist today.

   A current   B extinct   C modern   D present   E existing

13   Once the sugar dissolves into the water, it is impossible to ____ it from the liquid.

   A taste   B combine   C separate   D pour   E flavor

14   In the basement of the parking garage, there are signs on the escalator that ____ people to the exit on the second floor.

   A descend   B drive   C lower   D stop   E lead

15   The comedian used funny gestures to ____ the audience while telling his jokes.

   A entertain   B bore   C annoy   D bother   E upset

16 To win the debate, she had to ____ strong arguments with facts and evidence.

(A) support   (B) reject   (C) fake   (D) forget   (E) pretend

17 The criminal tried to ____ his own tracks, but the detective still found evidence.

(A) reveal   (B) explain   (C) display   (D) cover   (E) identify

18 The ____ applause made the surprised singer smile with joy.

(A) required   (B) single   (C) absent   (D) predicted   (E) unexpected

19 His outfit was so ____ that people kept staring at him as he walked down the sidewalk.

(A) common   (B) normal   (C) peculiar   (D) plain   (E) dull

20 The explorers gazed across the ____ desert that stretched endlessly to the horizon.

(A) enclosed   (B) vast   (C) narrow   (D) compact   (E) limited

- End of Practice Test 3. -
- The Answer Key begins on the next page. -

ANSWER KEY FOR PRACTICE TEST 1 (WORKBOOK FORMAT)

Verbal Analogies, Practice Test 1

1. A. Soft is the opposite of hard. Deep is the opposite of shallow.
2. D. A microscope is used by a scientist. A whistle is used by a referee.
3. C. A deck contains multiple cards. A flower contains multiple petals.
4. E. An hour is part of a day. A word is part of a sentence.
5. B. A cow provides milk. A sheep provides wool.
6. A. Scissors are used to cut. A sponge is used to wipe.
7. C. Jogging is a form of running. Strolling is a form of walking.
8. C. Chilly is a lesser degree of freezing. Misty is a lesser degree of foggy.
9. D. A bow is used with an arrow. A hammer is used with a nail.
10. E. A violin is a type of instrument. A rose is a type of flower.
11. A. A saw is used to cut. A needle is used to stitch.
12. D. An author is someone who writes. A baker is someone who cooks.
13. E. You pour water. You spend money.
14. A. A feather is part of a bird. A city is part of a state.
15. C. Silent means very quiet. Starving means very hungry.
16. B. A whale is a type of mammal. A lizard is a type of reptile.
17. E. A lock is used with a key. Toothpaste is used with a toothbrush.
18. C. Dusk is the opposite of dawn. Entrance is the opposite of exit.
19. D. Fire produces smoke. The sun produces heat.
20. B. Something very bright is glowing. Something very dim is dark.
21. D. A pen is used to write. Chalk is used to draw.
22. E. Win is the opposite of lose. Grow is the opposite of shrink.

Verbal Classification, Practice Test 1

1. B. A sunflower is a type of flower, like a rose, tulip, and daisy.
2. C. A paintbrush is a tool used for adding color, like a pencil, marker, and crayon.
3. E. A candle produces heat and light, like the Sun, a fire, and lava.
4. A. A cello is a type of string instrument, like a guitar, harp, and violin.
5. D. A spoon is a utensil used for eating, like a fork, knife, and chopsticks.
6. D. A jaguar is a big cat, like a lion, tiger, and leopard.
7. D. New York is a city, like Paris, London, and Rome.
8. E. A recliner is a type of seating furniture, like a couch, chair, and stool.

Verbal Classification, Practice Test 1, continued

9. B. Jupiter is a planet, like Mercury, Venus, and Earth.

10. E. A rectangle is a shape, like a square, triangle, and circle.

11. B. A dentist is a medical professional, like a doctor, nurse, and surgeon.

12. D. A seal is a marine animal, like a shark, whale, and dolphin.

13. B. A saw is a hand tool, like a hammer, wrench, and screwdriver.

14. A. A ridge is a landform that rises above the ground, like a mountain, hill, and volcano.

15. C. A pear is a fruit that grows on a tree, like a cherry, lemon, and apple.

16. E. A sheriff is a law enforcement officer, like a detective, police officer, and security guard.

17. D. A trout is a type of fish, like a goldfish, tuna, and salmon.

18. C. A pine is a type of tree, just as an oak, elm, and maple.

19. A. A day is a time measurement unit, just as an hour, minute, and second.

20. D. The Arctic is a cold region, like the North Pole, Antarctica, and Alaska.

21. E. Cheerful is an emotion associated with happiness, just as happy, joyful, and excited are.

22. E. Soccer is a sport, just like tennis, basketball, and golf.

Sentence Completion, Practice Test 1

1. B. Baby birds make noise when they need something. If they are hungry, they are calling for food.

2. C. A bright sun can make it hard to see. To cover your eyes means to block light from the eyes.

3. E. People wear jackets when it is not warm. "Chilly" means the temperature is low.

4. A. Rain can make surfaces wet. The only answer choice that would make the path slippery is the rain.

5. B. Without a map, explorers could have a hard time finding their way. "Lost" is the only answer choice that fits.

6. D. Since Leo is fixing a light, he must go up the ladder. "Climbed" means moving upward, which makes the most sense. The word "despite" is important because it means he did something even though he was afraid. Since he has a fear of heights, the only action that makes sense is climbing the ladder anyway.

7. B. A detective must look carefully at clues. "Examined" means to study something closely.

8. A. After training, a person would participate in a race. "Completed" means to finish. You wouldn't train for months to do any of the other answer choices.

9. E. The problem was done correctly, so there was no reason to ask for help "Solved" means finding the right answer.

10. C. The wind blows leaves in different directions. "Scattered" means spreading things around randomly.

11. D. Rain would make camping difficult. "Postpone" means to schedule something off for a later date.

12. C. She doesn't want others to see her excitement. "Conceal" means to hide something or keep something from being noticed.

13. B. The highest point of a mountain is called a "summit." All the other words have to do with low points or the bottom of the mountain. You would not climb up to reach these.

14. B. The warning of thunder means a storm is coming. "Forming" means starting to grow or come together.

15. A. He needed to stay calm. "Controlled" means staying in charge of feelings.

16. E. Scientists would redo experiments to make sure they have correct results. Also, while some scientists invent things, "invent" is not the correct answer here. "Confirm" means to make sure something is true or correct.

17. D. Sorting puzzle pieces helps make solving easier. "Organize" means to arrange in order.

18. B. The teacher needs to make sure students understand the instructions before starting the test. "Explained" means giving clear details, which makes the most sense.

19. B. Since he wants to avoid dropping the vase, he must be holding it. "Lifted" means he picked it up carefully, which fits best.

20. C. "Extinguish" means to stop a fire from burning. Firefighters put out fires with hoses. ("Escape" is not correct because hoses would not be used by firefighters to escape from a fire.)

ANSWER KEY FOR PRACTICE TEST 2

Verbal Analogies, Practice Test 2

1. A. A lion roars. A frog croaks. (This is the sound the animal makes.)

2. E. A buckle fastens a belt. A button fastens a shirt.

3. B. Texas is a state. Asia is a continent.

4. C. A ruler measures length. A clock measures time.

5. B. A beak is part of a bird. A hoof is part of a goat.

6. D. An ocean is larger than a sea. A canyon is larger than a valley.

7. C. A dolphin is related to a whale. (They are both mammals that live in the sea.) A goldfish is related to a guppy. (They are both smaller fish that are often found in aquariums.)

8. D. A gram measures weight. A meter measures distance.

9. E. Eyes are used to see. A nose is used to smell.

10. E. A bicycle is a slower version of a motorcycle. A motorcycle has an engine. A wagon is a slower version of a truck. A truck has an engine.

11. D. An orchestra is led by a conductor. A ship's crew is led by a captain.

12. B. A phone runs on a battery. A refrigerator runs on electricity.

13. C. "Knight" and "night" are homophones. "Flour" and "flower" are homophones.

14. A. A chapter is part of a book. An actor is part of a cast.

15. B. Seaweed is found in the ocean. A cactus is found in the desert.

16. D. Warm is a lesser degree of hot. (Something very, very warm is hot.) Breezy is a lesser degree of windy. (When it's very, very breezy, it's windy.)

17. C. A teacher is in charge of a classroom. A mayor is in charge of a city.

18. C. A bee is part of a swarm. A star is part of a galaxy.

19. A. Push is the opposite of pull. Rise is the opposite of fall.

20. E. Orange is the color of a carrot. Brown is the color of honey.

21. B. A director is responsible for a movie and oversees that it goes well. A pilot is responsible for a flight and oversees that the flight goes well.

22. E. A sundial is an old way to tell time, and a clock is a more modern way of doing so. A compass is an old way to find directions/find your way, and a GPS is a more modern way of doing so.

Verbal Classification, Practice Test 2

1. D. Orange is a color, like red, blue, and green.
2. D. A cottage is a type of home, like an apartment, cabin, and mansion.
3. A. Korean is a language, like Spanish, German, and Japanese.
4. B. Feeling is a sense, like touching, smelling, and tasting.
5. C. A stopwatch is used to measure time, like an alarm clock, grandfather clock, and an hourglass.
6. E. Gloves are clothing items worn on hands, like mittens, rings, and bracelets.
7. D. A freeway is used for driving, just as a highway, street, and road.
8. C. A meteor is an object found in space, like a moon, comet, and planet.
9. A. A mug holds liquid and is used for drinking, just as a cup, thermos, and bottle. (A straw does not belong because it is not a container used for drinking.)
10. C. The Arctic is an ocean, like the Atlantic, Pacific, and Indian.
11. B. A trail is used for walking, just like a sidewalk, path, and crosswalk.
12. C. Chuckling is a happy sound, like laughing, smiling, and giggling.
13. E. Socks are worn on feet, like skates, shoes, and stockings.
14. D. A leopard is a big cat, like a lion, tiger, and cheetah.
15. E. A cherry is a kind of produce (fruit/vegetable) that comes in a group, like grapes, bananas, and tomatoes.
16. A. Sprint is a way of moving quickly, just like jog, skip, and run.
17. B. Sit is a "still" position, just like stand, rest, and lean.
18. B. A robin is a type of bird, just like a peacock, ostrich, and hawk.
19. E. Coffee is a liquid, like juice, vinegar, and syrup.
20. D. An oyster is an animal with a shell, just like a turtle, clam, and snail.

Sentence Completion, Practice Test 2

1. B. The wind is strong enough to break branches. "Powerful" means very strong, which makes the most sense.
2. A. Forgetting details would be a "loss" in memory. (The other choices would make one's memory get better.)
3. C. Mangoes contain "nutrients," which help keep people healthy.
4. D. Borrowing money means you must "repay" it (pay it back) over time.
5. E. "Bustling" means full of busy activity and energy. A clue here is the word "unlike." The city is unlike a village.
6. C. The designs of ice crystals and snowflakes follow math patterns. Note the words "symmetry" and "hexagon." "Mathematical" means related to numbers and shapes. ("Colorful" doesn't work because both objects appear white/clear.)

7. A. The walls were built to stop people from getting in. "Prevent" means to keep something from happening.

8. D. If a park is closed, people would be frustrated, especially if they had rushed to the park.

9. C. A public event is one that anyone can attend. (Note that it cannot be "free" because you have to buy a ticket.)

10. D. "Incredible" means amazing or hard to believe. Because seeing the Grand Canyon was beyond anything the person could have imagined, the other choices would not work.

11. A. "Conserve" means to save and use carefully so it doesn't run out.

12. E. "Unusual" means not common or different from what is normal.

13. A. "Ancestor" means a family member from the past.

14. B. "Permanent" means something will last and not change.

15. B. Penguins live in very cold places. "Survive" means to stay alive in difficult conditions.

16. D. "Deserted" means empty and without people.

17. C. If two areas are "connected," they are linked together.

18. E. "Approval" means permission or a way of saying yes or agreeing to something.

19. B. The lake got bigger because of heavy rain. "Expand" means to grow or increase in size.

20. A. A captain must "steer" to guide the ship.

ANSWER KEY FOR PRACTICE TEST 3

Verbal Analogies, Practice Test 3

1. B. A chef works in a kitchen. A doctor works at a hospital.
2. A. You use your tongue to taste. You use your hand to touch. (The answer is not wave or clap because these are not one of the senses. Tasting and touching are two of the basic senses.)
3. D. Fur covers a bear. Scales cover a fish.
4. D. The Atlantic is an ocean next to the continent Europe. The Pacific is an ocean next to the continent of Asia. (Note that it can't be Canada and China because the answer must be a continent.)
5. B. A cube is a 3-D version of a square. A sphere is a 3-D version of a circle.
6. E. A roof is the top of a house. A peak is the top of a mountain.
7. A. An eagle and a falcon are both birds of prey. A whale and a dolphin are both marine mammals.
8. A. Liquid is measured in liters. Time is measured in minutes.
9. D. Happiness is the opposite of sadness. Huge is the opposite of tiny.
10. C. Narrow is the opposite of wide. Build is the opposite of destroy.
11. D. Canada and Mexico are both countries. India and China are both countries.
12. B. A rose is a type of flower. A maple is a type of tree.
13. C. A bat is a mammal. A crocodile is a reptile.
14. B. A train and a subway are similar forms of transport. A horse and a carriage are similar forms of transport.
15. A. A saw and a knife are both tools that cut. A microwave and an oven are both appliances that heat things up.
16. C. Fabric is made from cotton. Logs are made from a tree.
17. D. Single means one. Triple means three.
18. B. A grape grows on a vine. A cherry grows on a tree.
19. D. A letter goes in an envelope. Cereal goes in a bowl.
20. C. A poem is created by a poet. A painting is created by an painter.
21. A. Glasses are used to see. Headphones are used to listen.
22. E. Heat causes people to sweat. Cold causes people to shiver.

Verbal Classification, Practice Test 3

1. A. Europe is a continent, like North America, South America, and Africa.
2. B. Watermelons are fruits, like apples, bananas, and grapes.
3. D. A newspaper is something printed you read, like a book, magazine, and menu.

4. E. A knee is part of the leg, like an ankle, hip, and thigh.
5. A. A jacket is worn for warmth, like a scarf, hat, and mittens.
6. B. A year is a unit to measure time, like a week, day, and month.
7. D. A candle provides light, as does a flashlight, lantern, and headlamp.
8. C. A fairy is a mythical character (not a real person), like a mermaid, wizard, and witch.
9. A. These are all adjectives that describe various degrees of coldness.
10. B. These words all mean that something has been completed and is no longer continuing.
11. E. Chapter is a writing unit, like word, sentence, and paragraph.
12. D. These words all have similar meanings to "fast."
13. A. These are all things that travel in the air.
14. C. These are all words that are the lowest level.
15. D. These are all frozen forms of water (and cold).
16. E. These are all modes of transport that usually carry only one person.
17. E. These are all citrus fruits.
18. B. These are all vegetables.
19. D. These are all dairy products.
20. C. These are all things/people used to help keep something/someone safe.

Sentence Completion, Practice Test 3

1. C. "Tiny" means very small.
2. A. "Rate" refers to how fast something happens, like a river's flow.
3. D. "Approach" means moving closer.
4. E. As more people visit, small towns can grow into bigger places.
5. C. "Essential" means very important or necessary for life.
6. B. "Depend" means to count on someone for help.
7. B. To succeed on the exam, he must keep going. "Continue" means to keep doing something.
8. D. The climber needs to get stronger again. "Rebuild" means to build back up again, and here, to regain strength.
9. A. Pay attention to "even though" here. Often, people who are older are taller. Here, because of the use of "even though," the answer is "shortest." Also, people who are older are often thought to be wiser. Therefore, "wisest" is not the correct answer.
10. E. A bridge must be steady in the wind. "Firm" means strong and not moving easily.
11. A. "Extreme" means far beyond normal. People stay inside when it's very hot.
12. B. The scientist studies species that no longer exist. "Extinct" means completely gone.

13. C. Once sugar dissolves, it can't be easily removed. "Separate" means to keep things apart or not together.

14. E. "Lead" means to guide or show the way. Since the sentence mentions going from the basement to the second floor, the only logical answer is "lead." The other words would mean going down, staying in one place, or driving (which is not done on an escalator).

15. A. The comedian wants to keep the audience's attention. "Entertain" means to amuse or engage.

16. A. Strong arguments need facts. Here, "support" means to back up with evidence.

17. D. Someone trying to hide evidence would "cover" their tracks.

18. E. The singer didn't expect the applause. (The singer was "surprised.") "Unexpected" means something happened as a surprise.

19. C. His outfit stood out and attracted attention. "Peculiar" means unusual or strange, which makes the most sense.

20. B. The desert is described as stretching endlessly, meaning it is very large. "Vast" means very big or wide.

Need more practice?

- Get **300+ <u>new</u> questions** per book!

- Check out more **Savant Test Prep**™ books on Amazon®.

www.ingramcontent.com/pod-product-compliance
Lightning Source LLC
Chambersburg PA
CBHW081725120626
46550CB00010B/3250